Wings and Scales

A Coloring Book

By Rohvannyn Shaw

www.rohvannynshaw.com

For Shinseiko

ISBN-13: 978-1530761524
ISBN-10: 1530761522

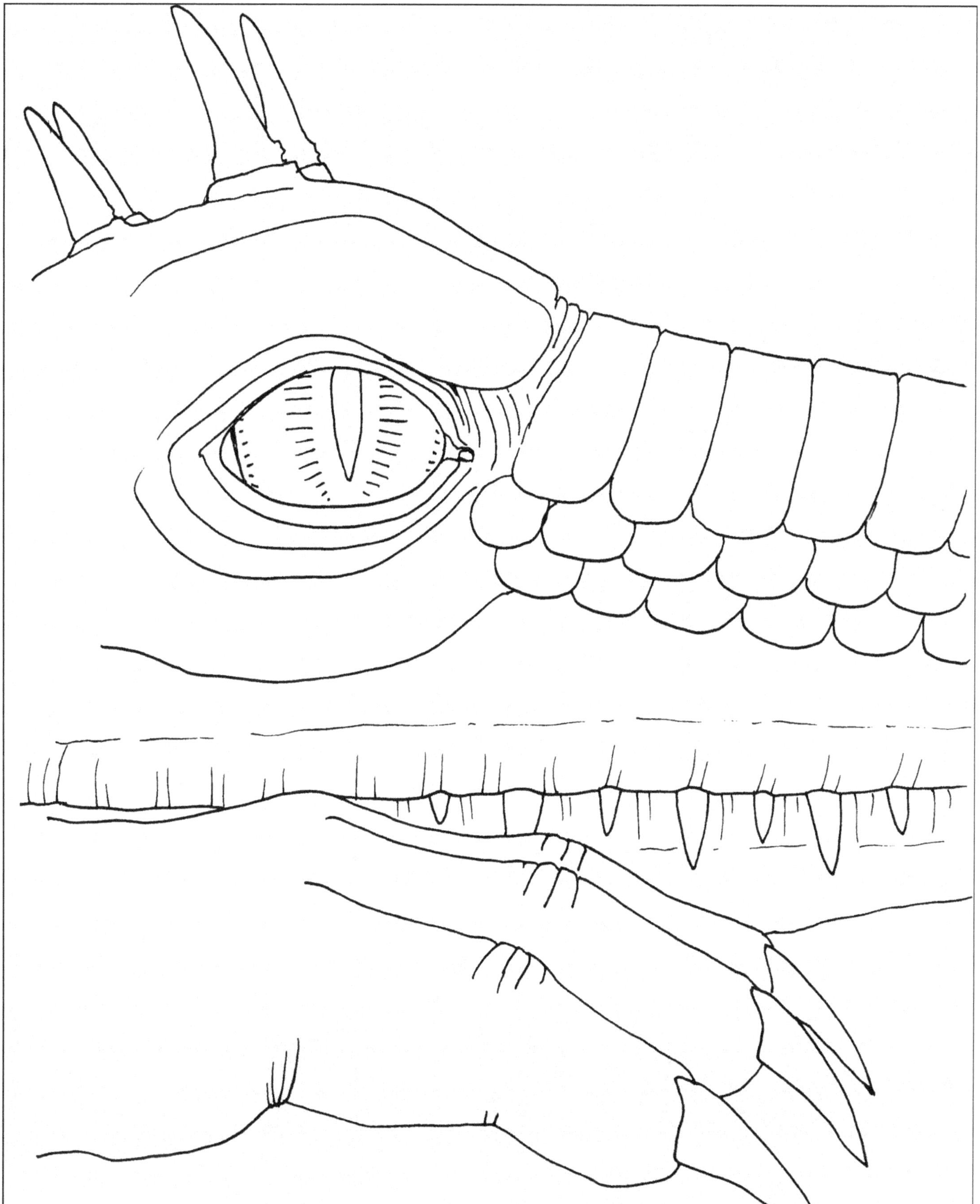

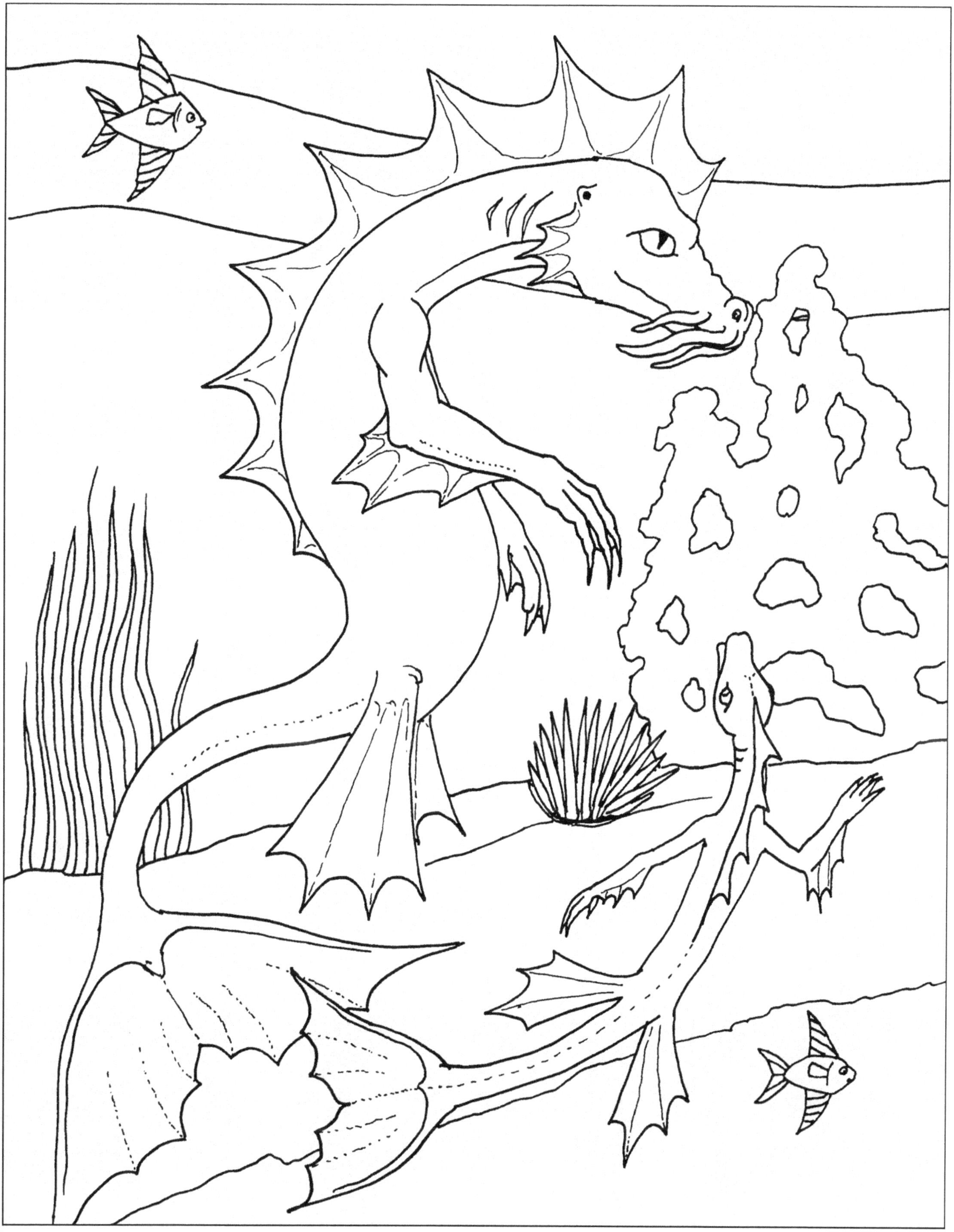

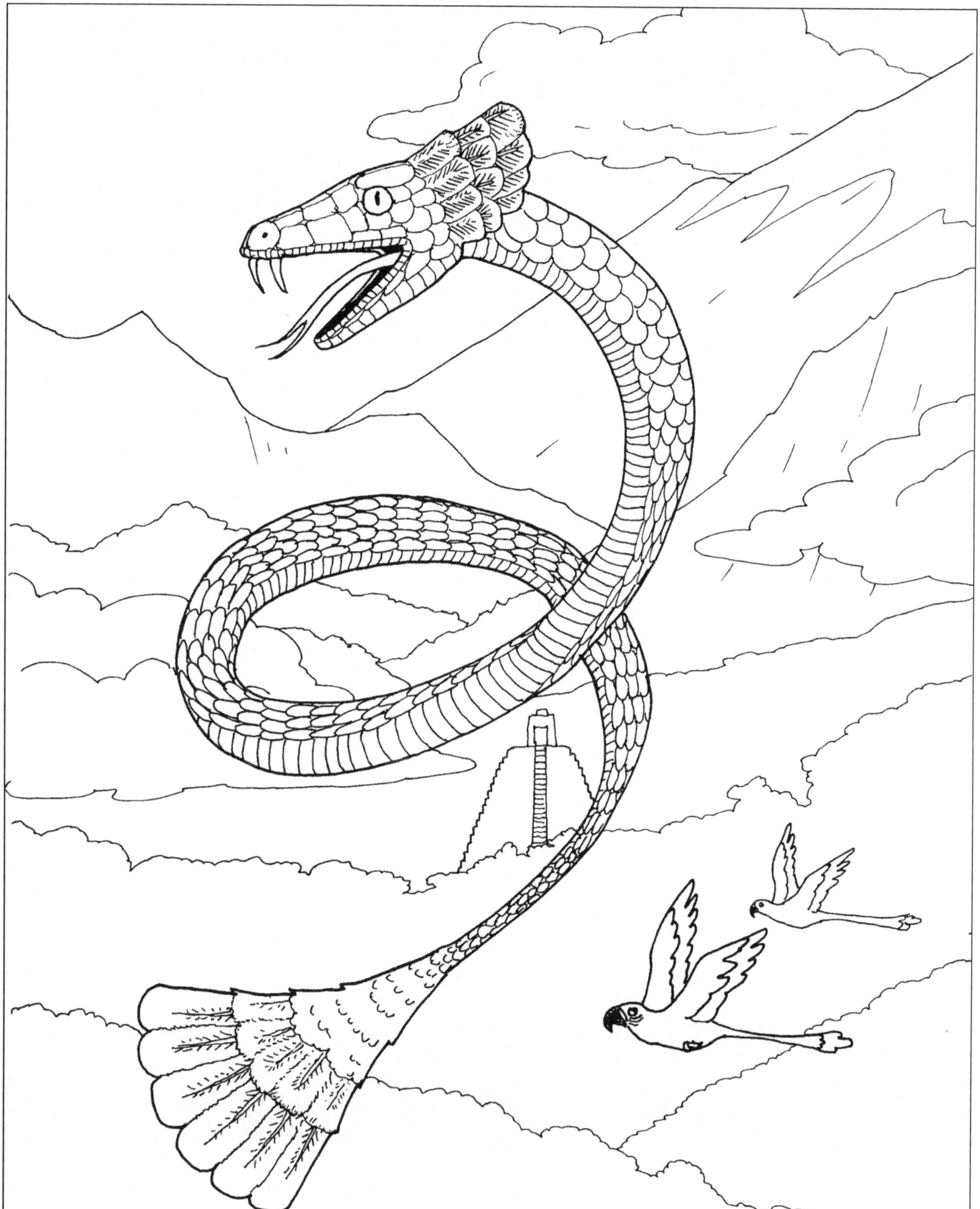

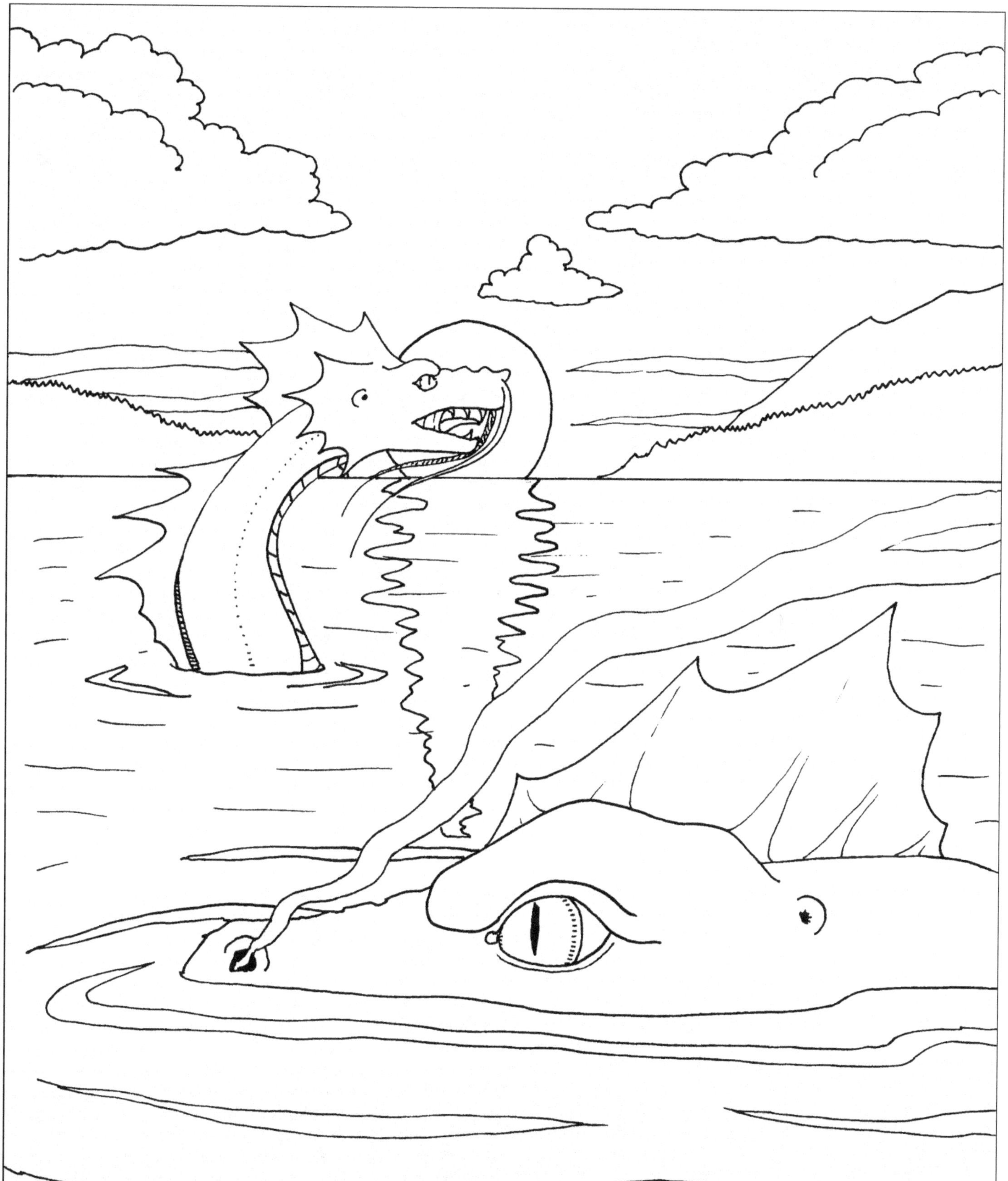

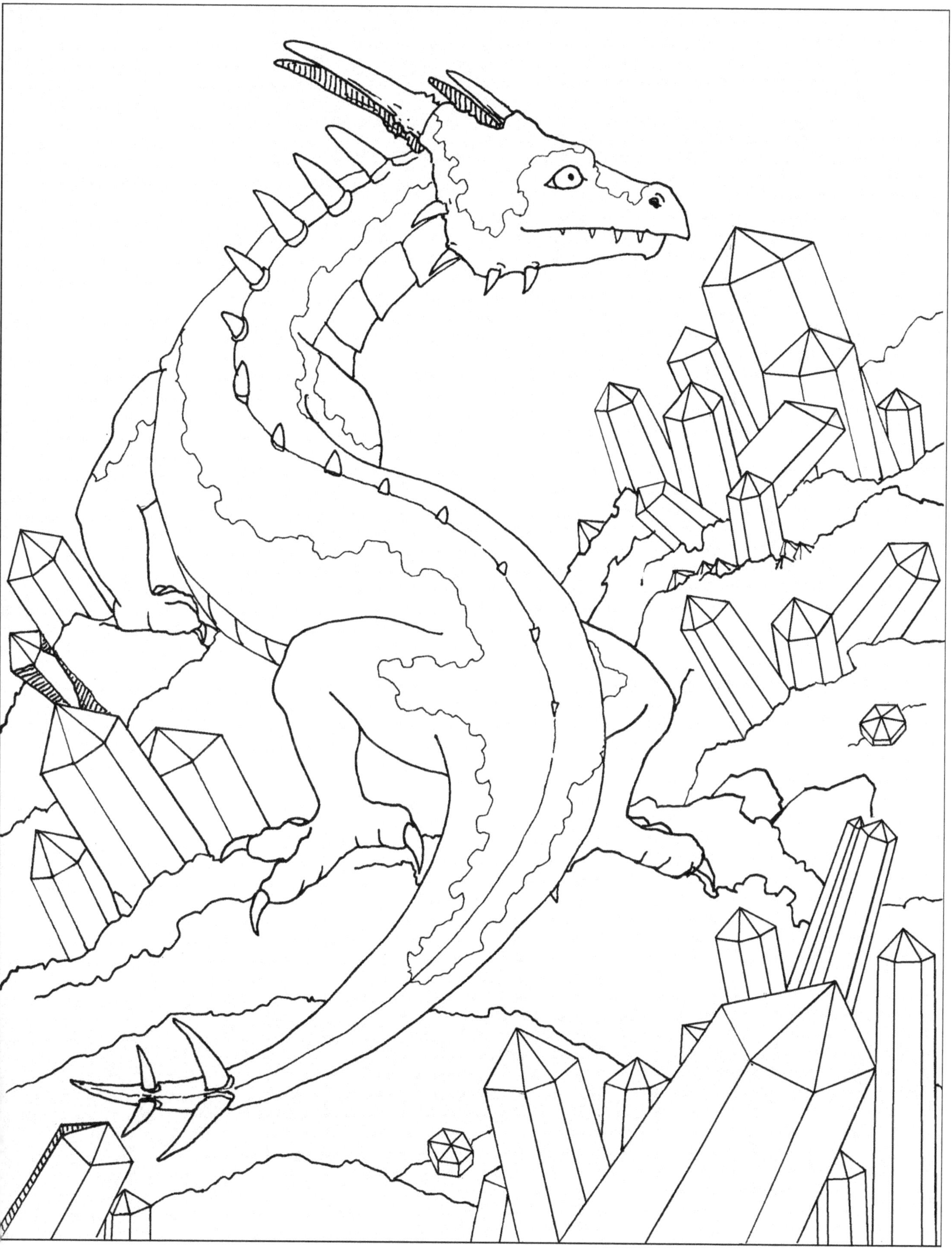

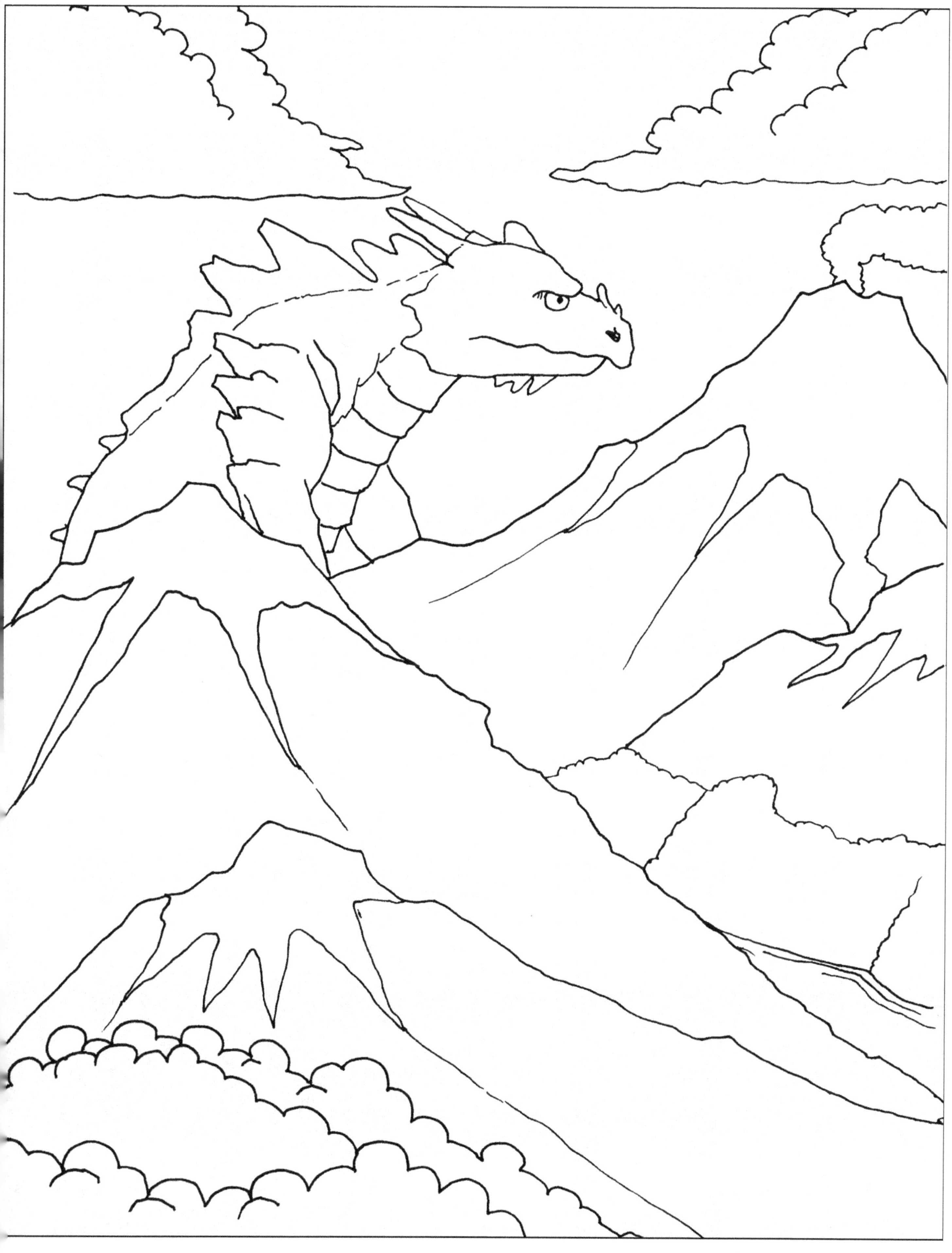

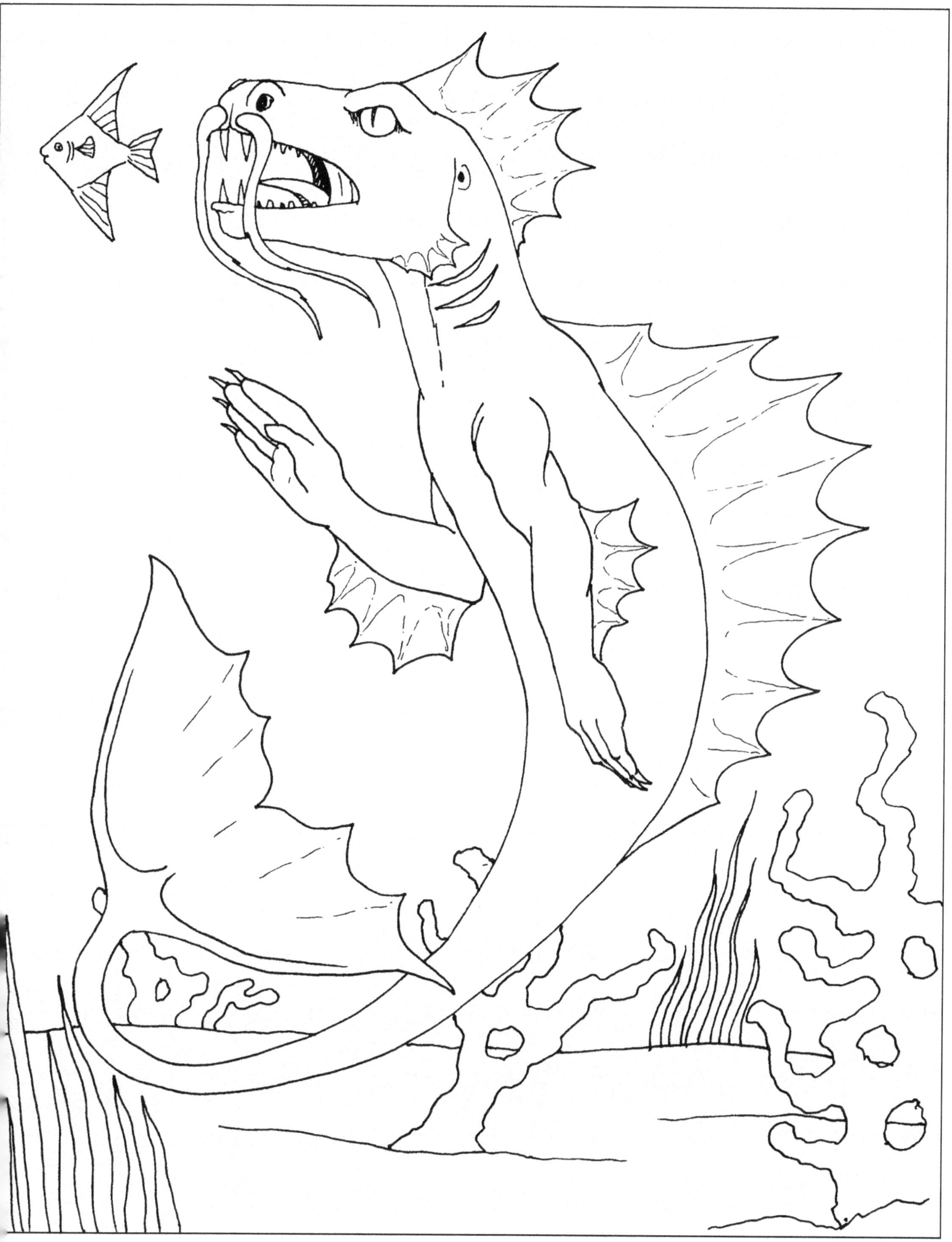

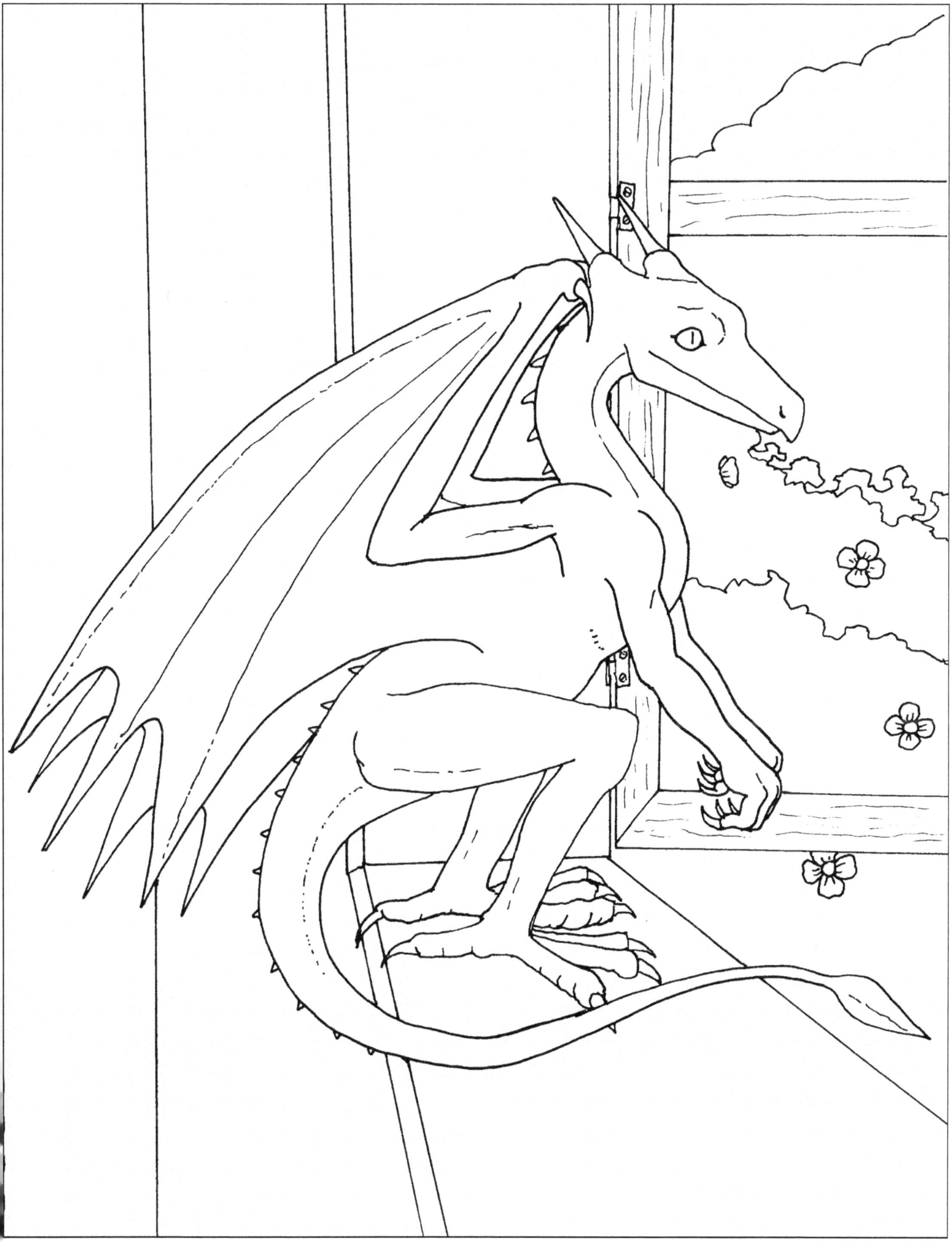

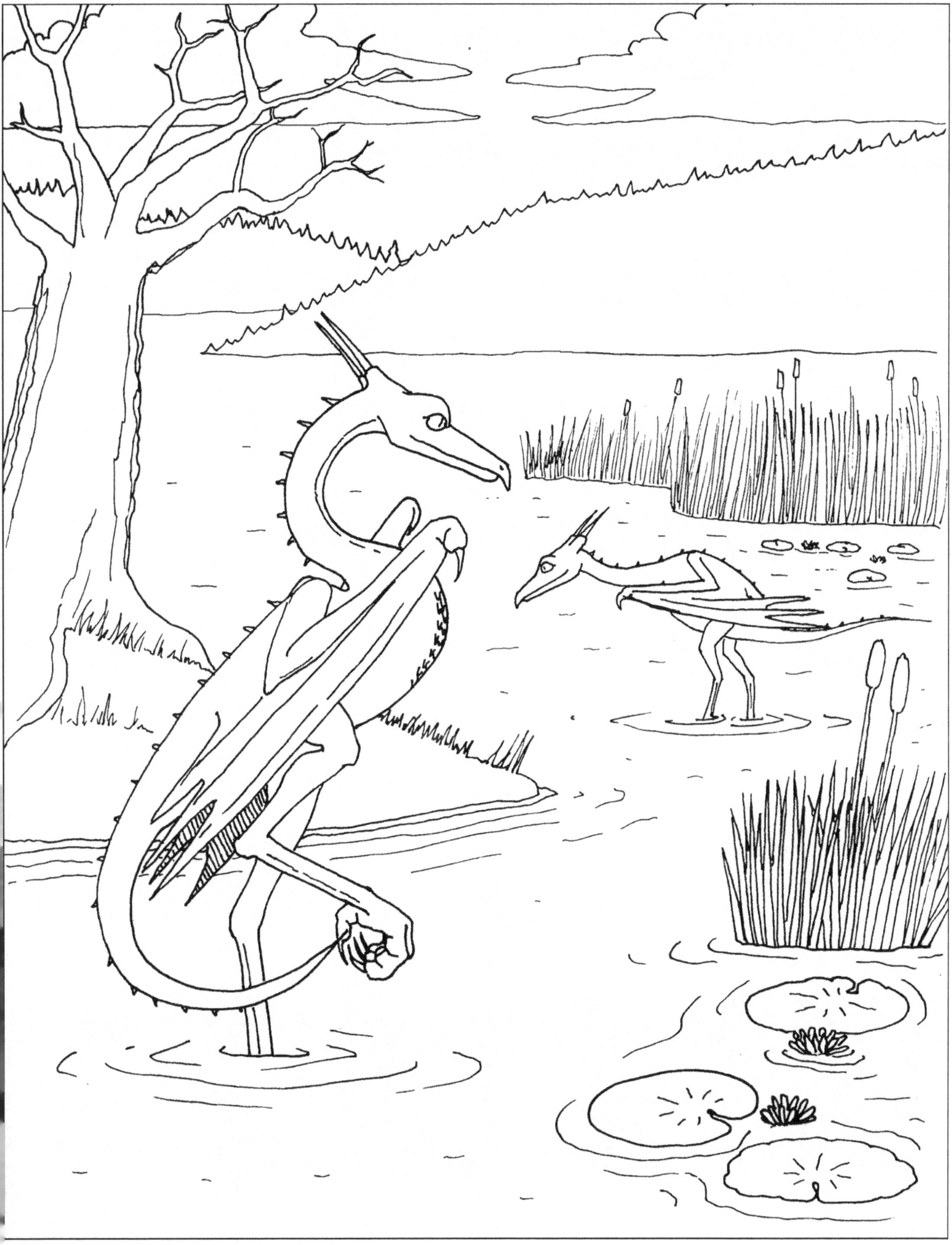

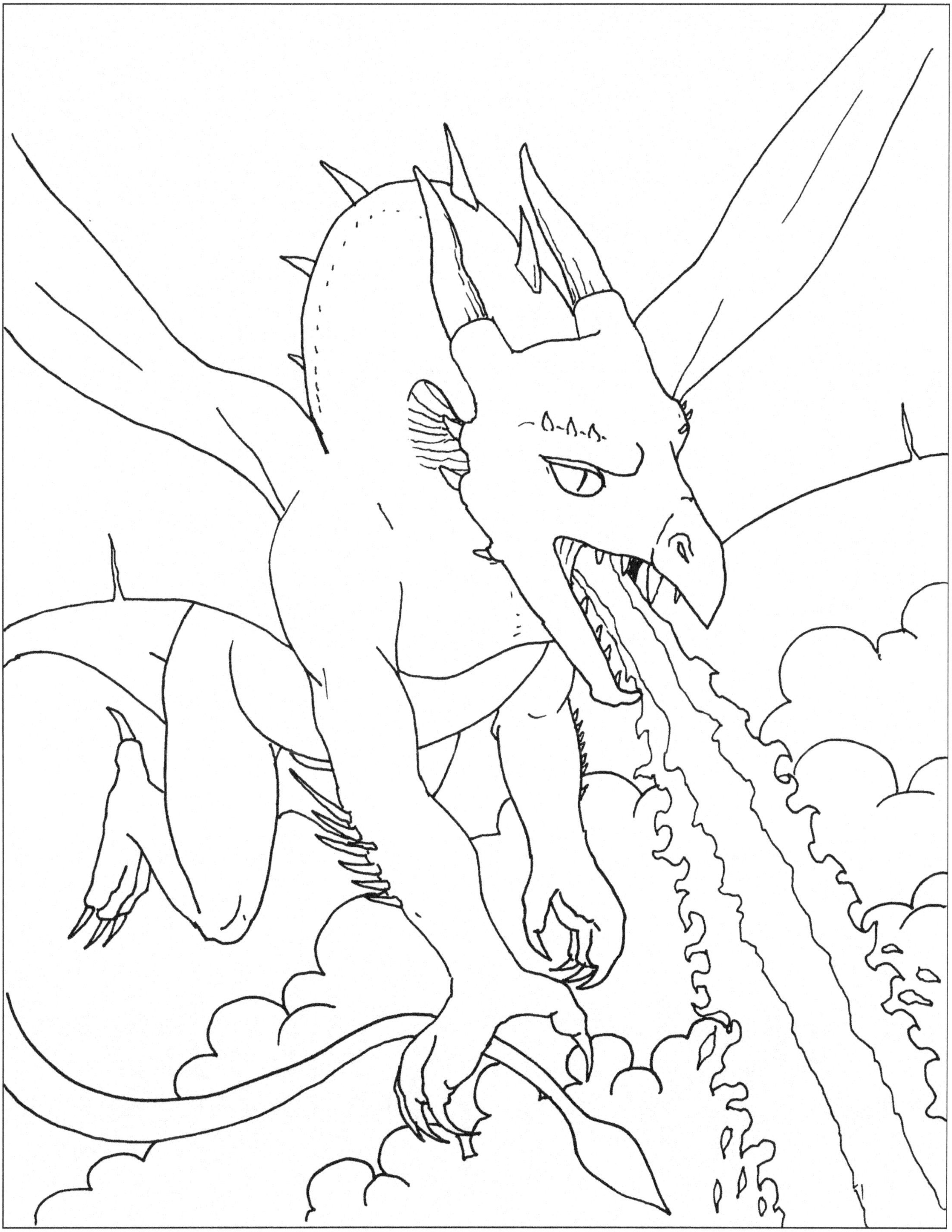

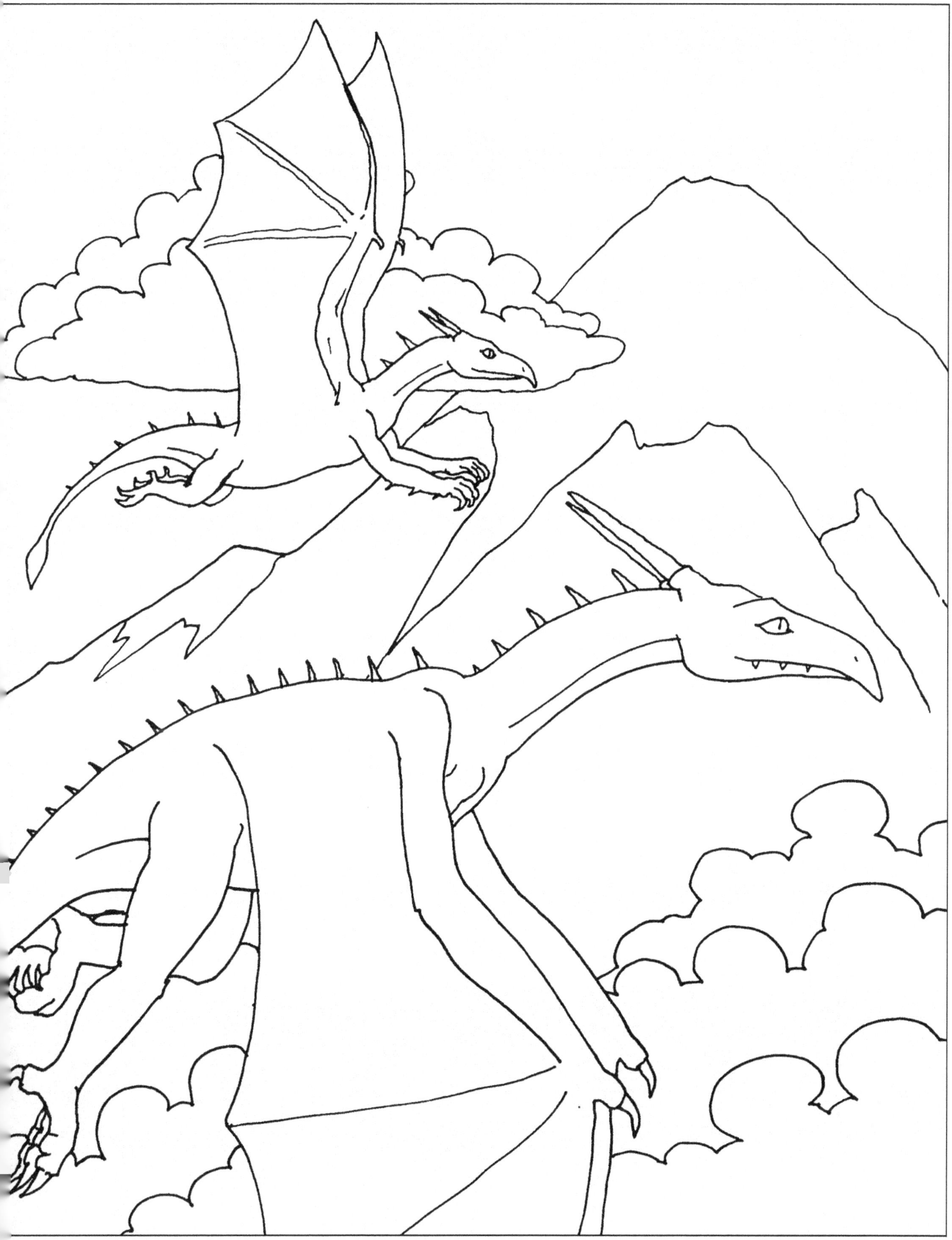

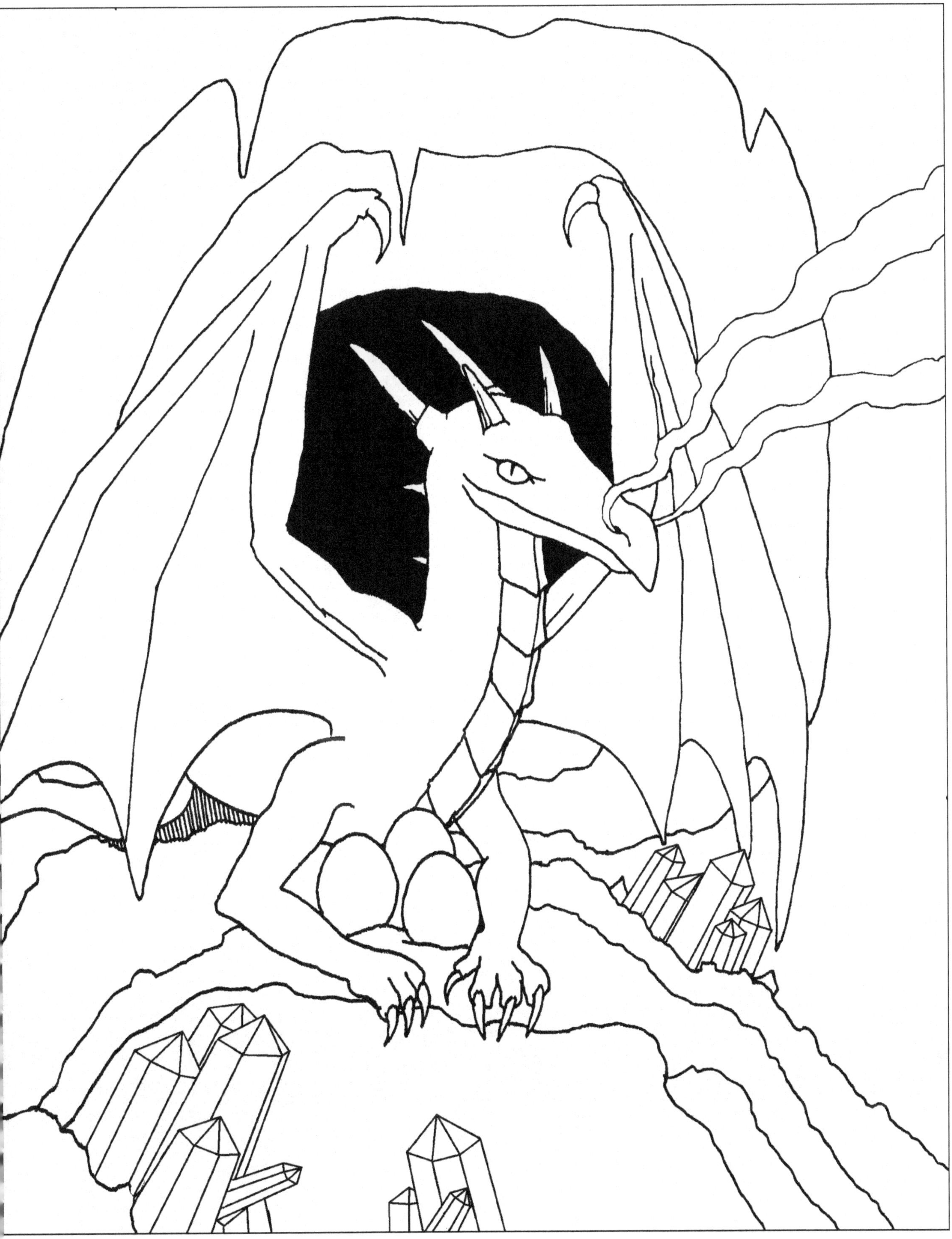

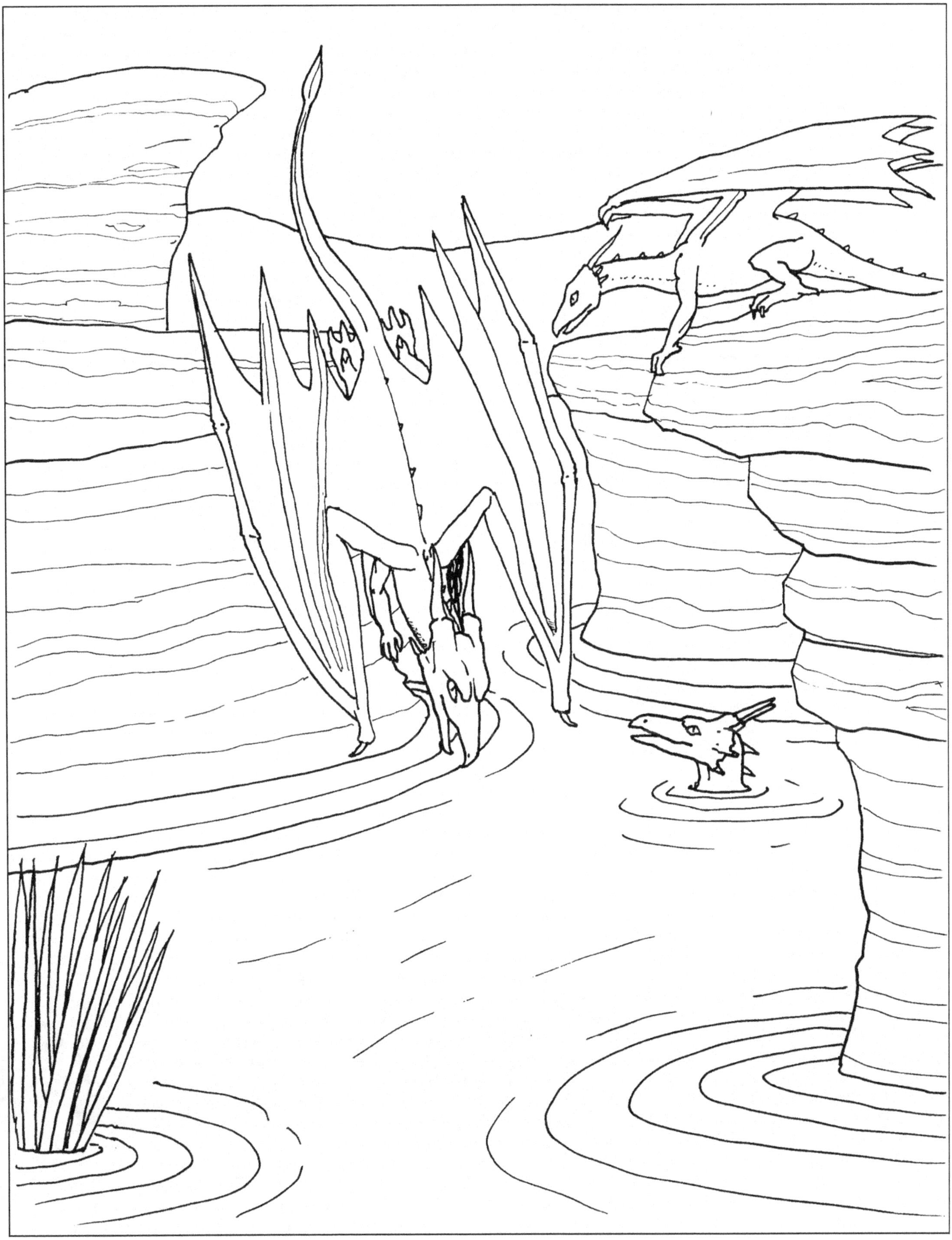

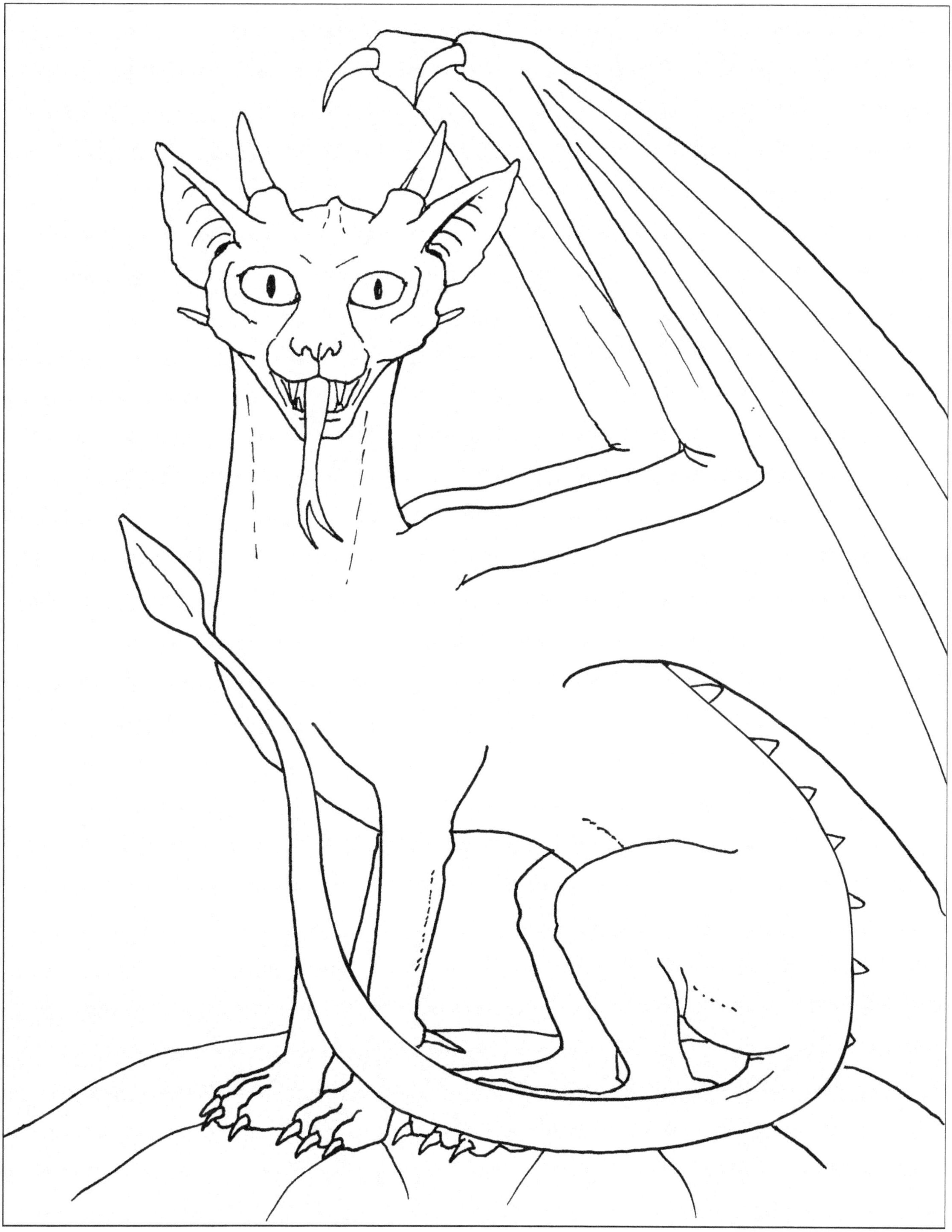

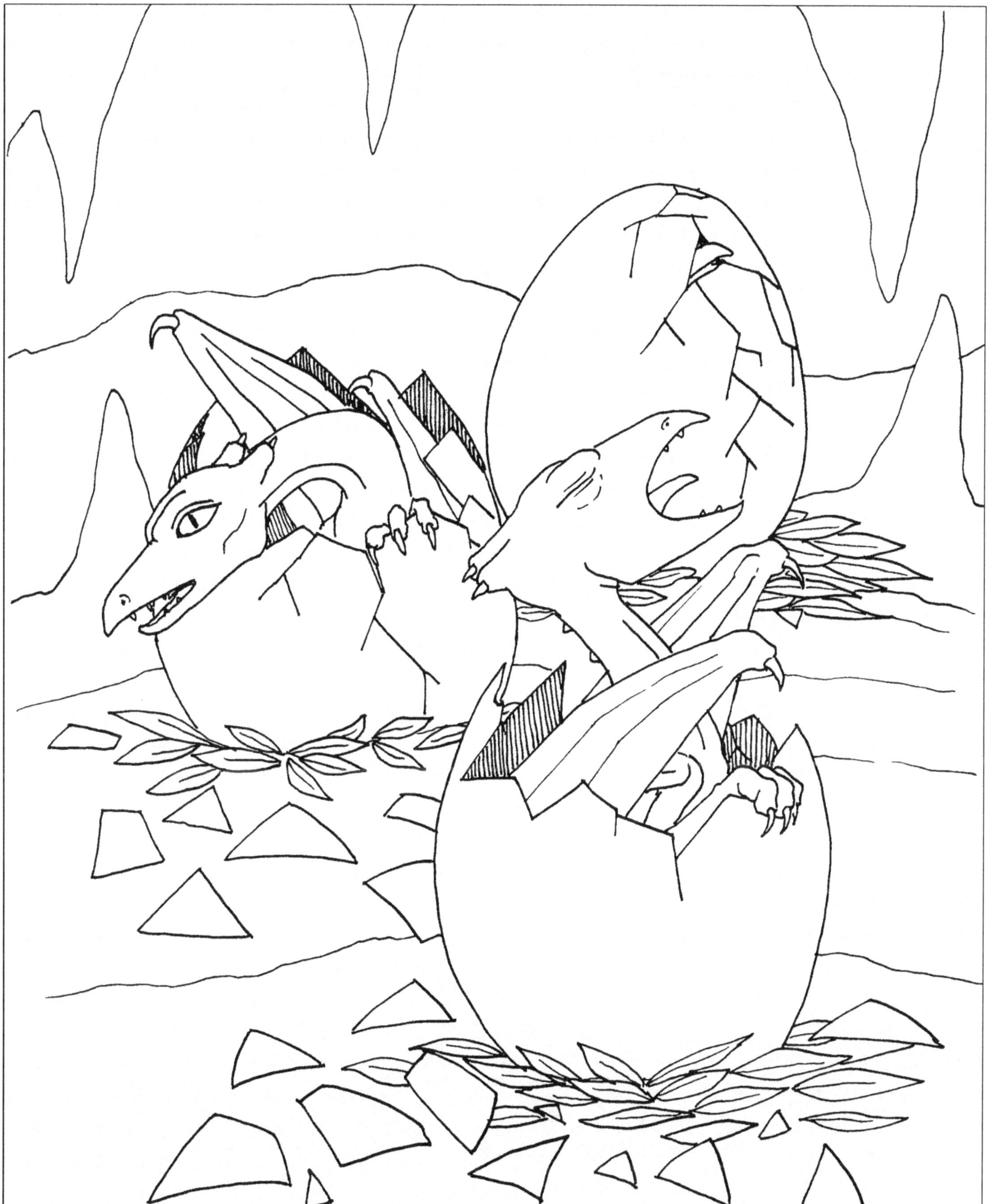

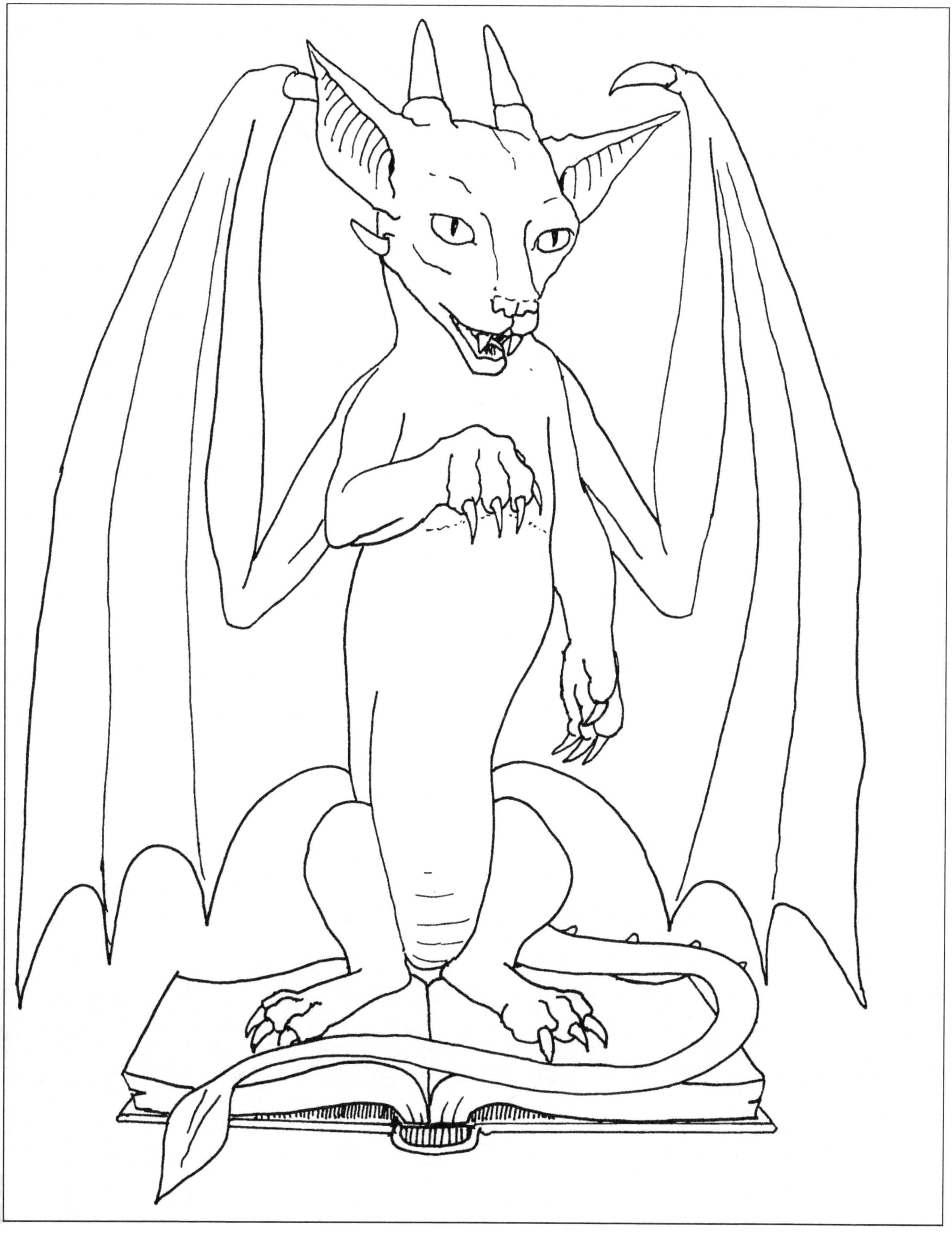

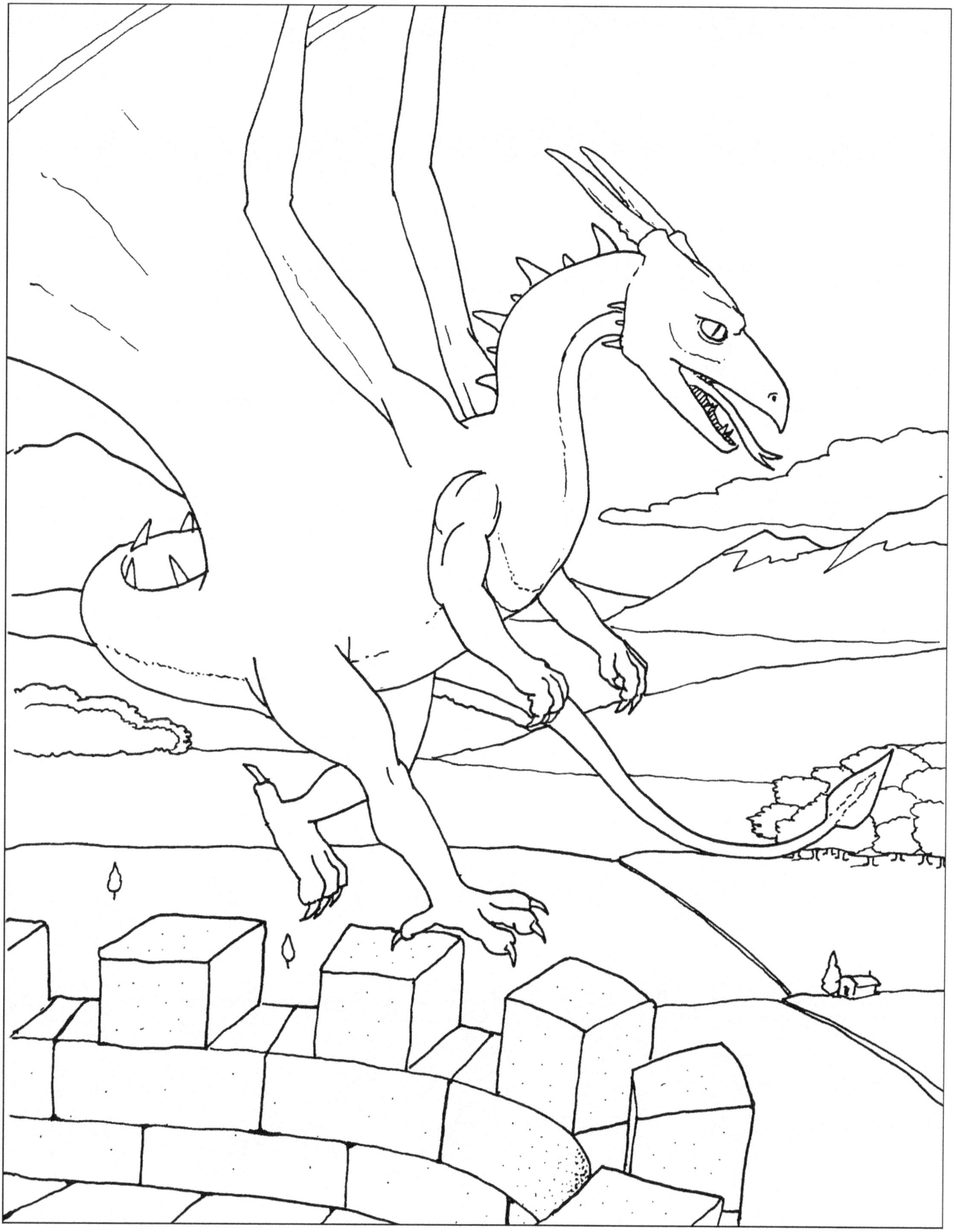

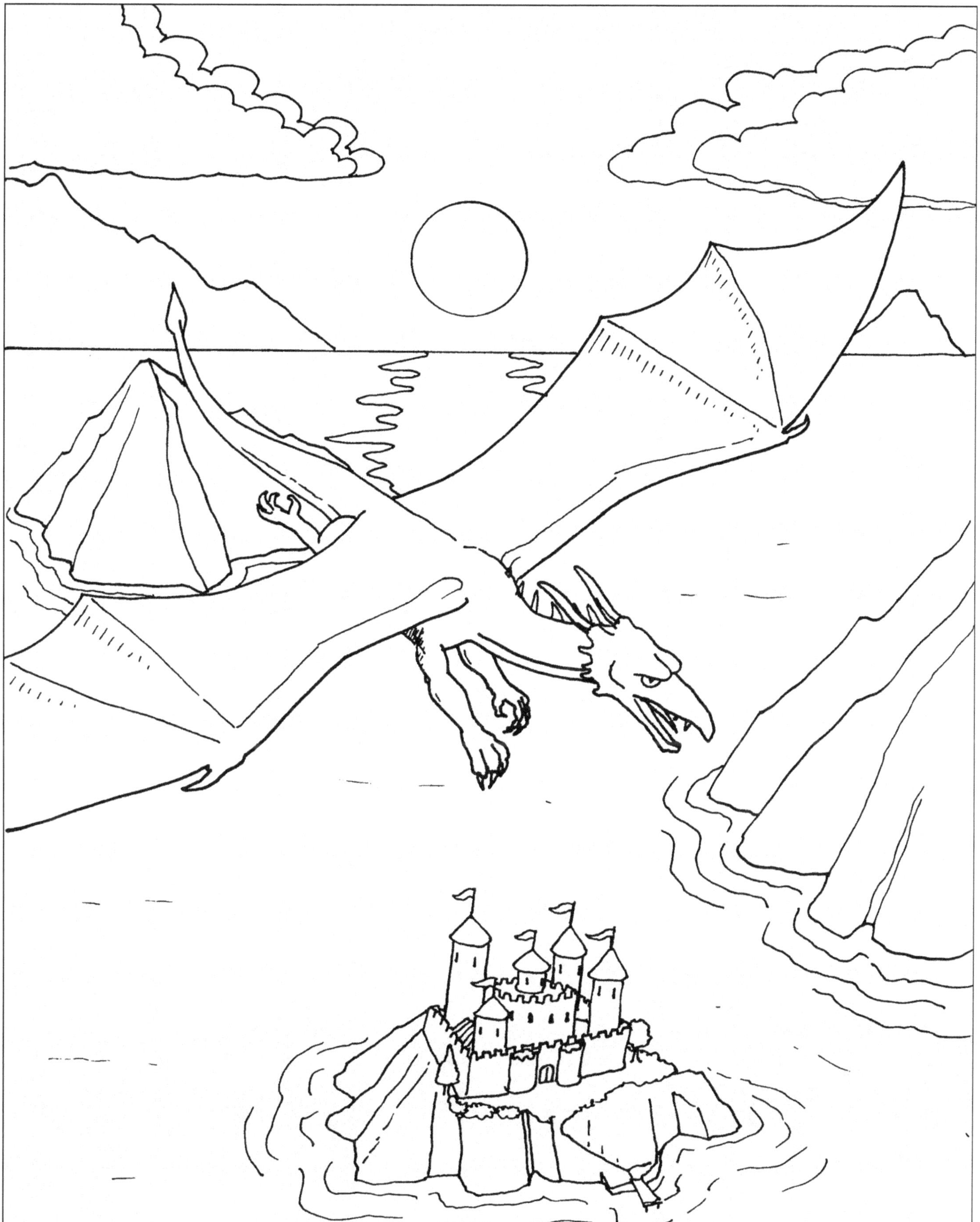

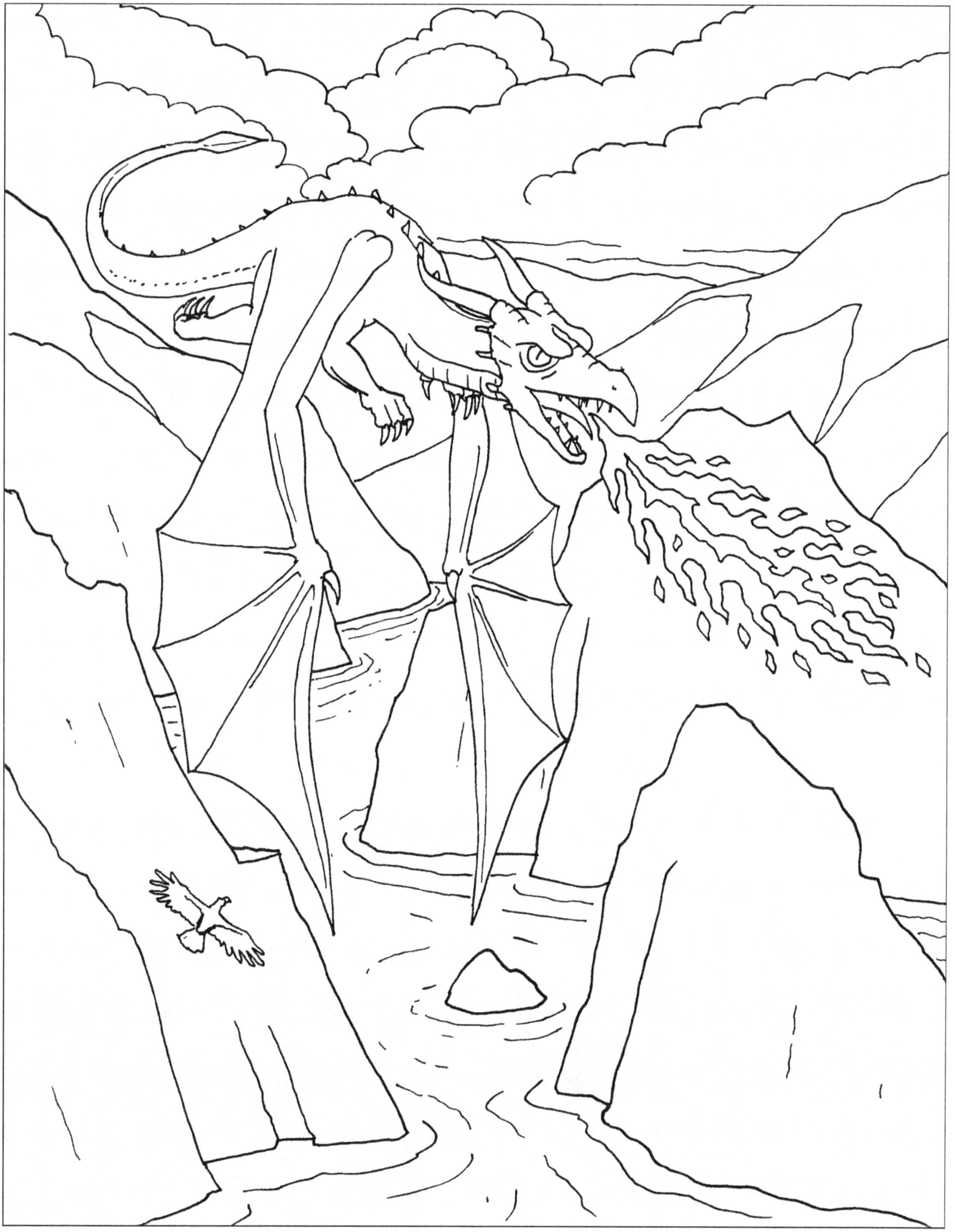

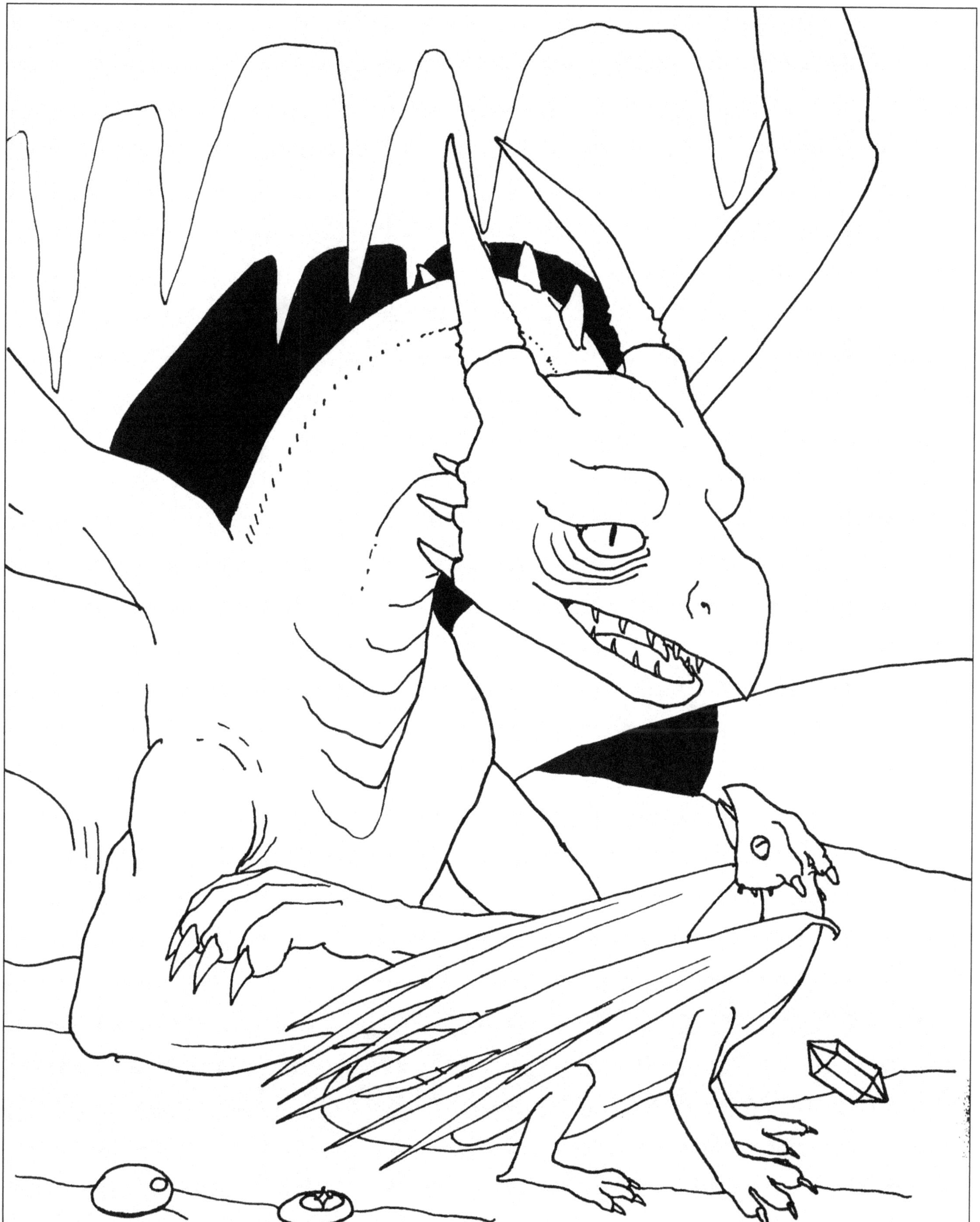

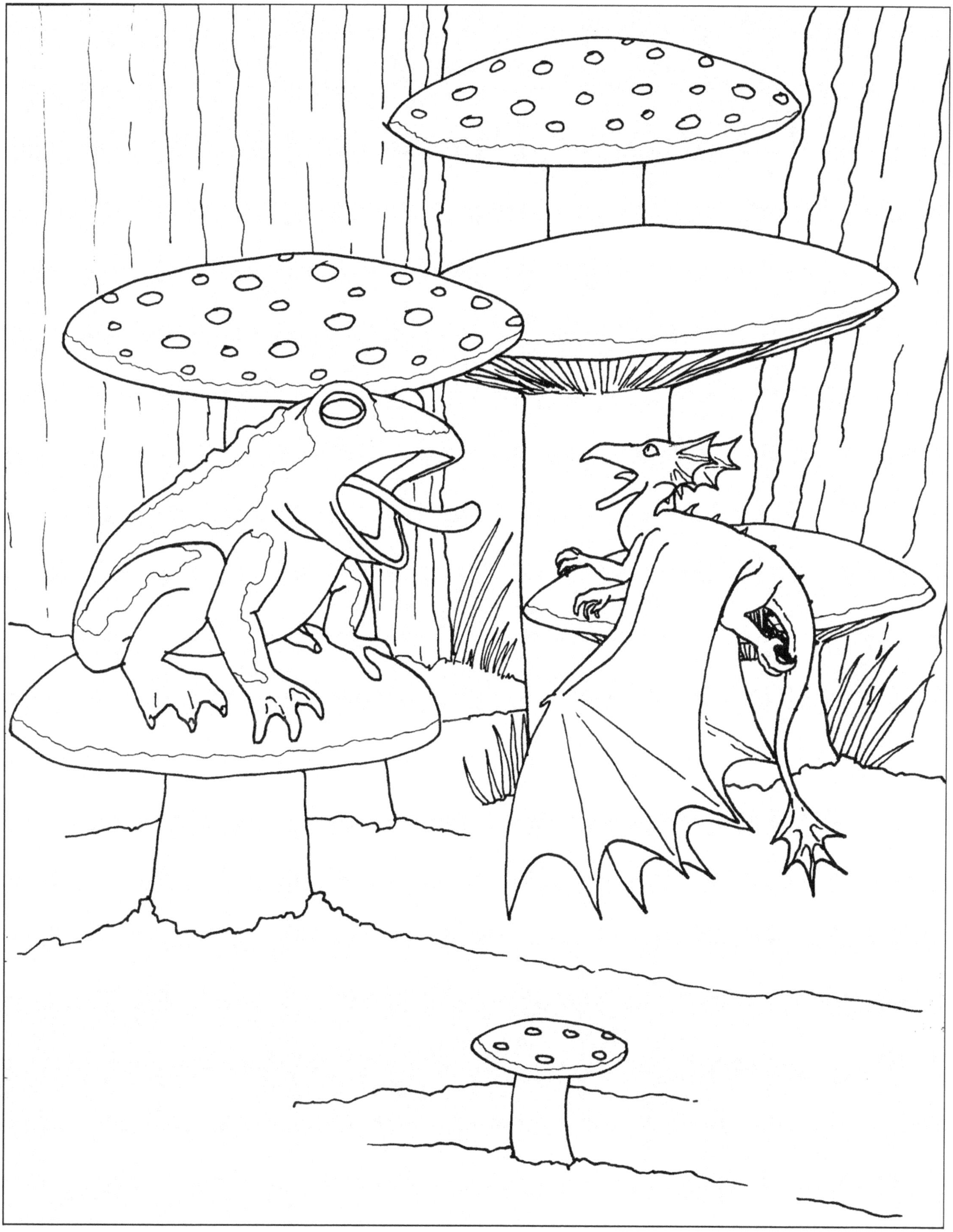

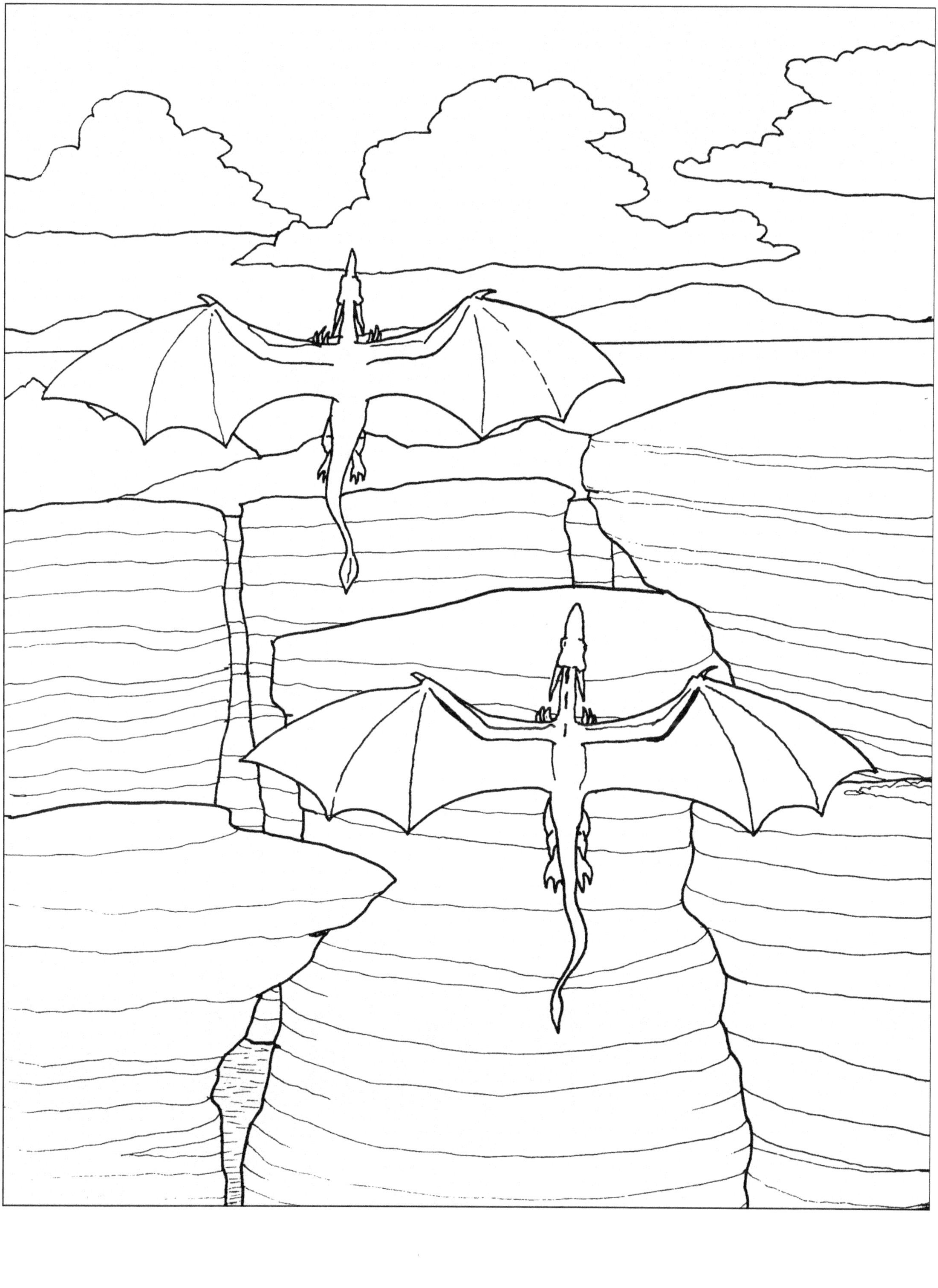

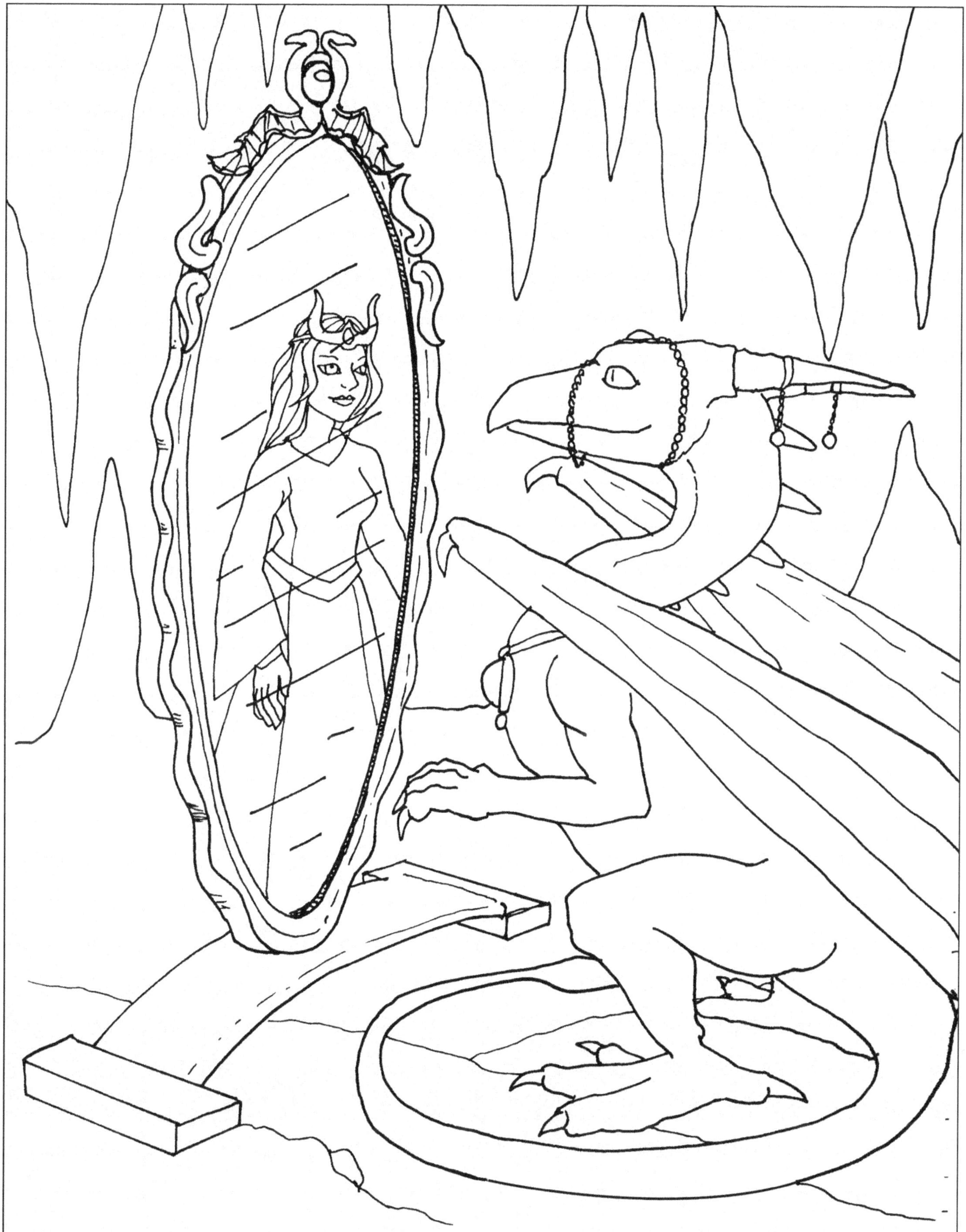

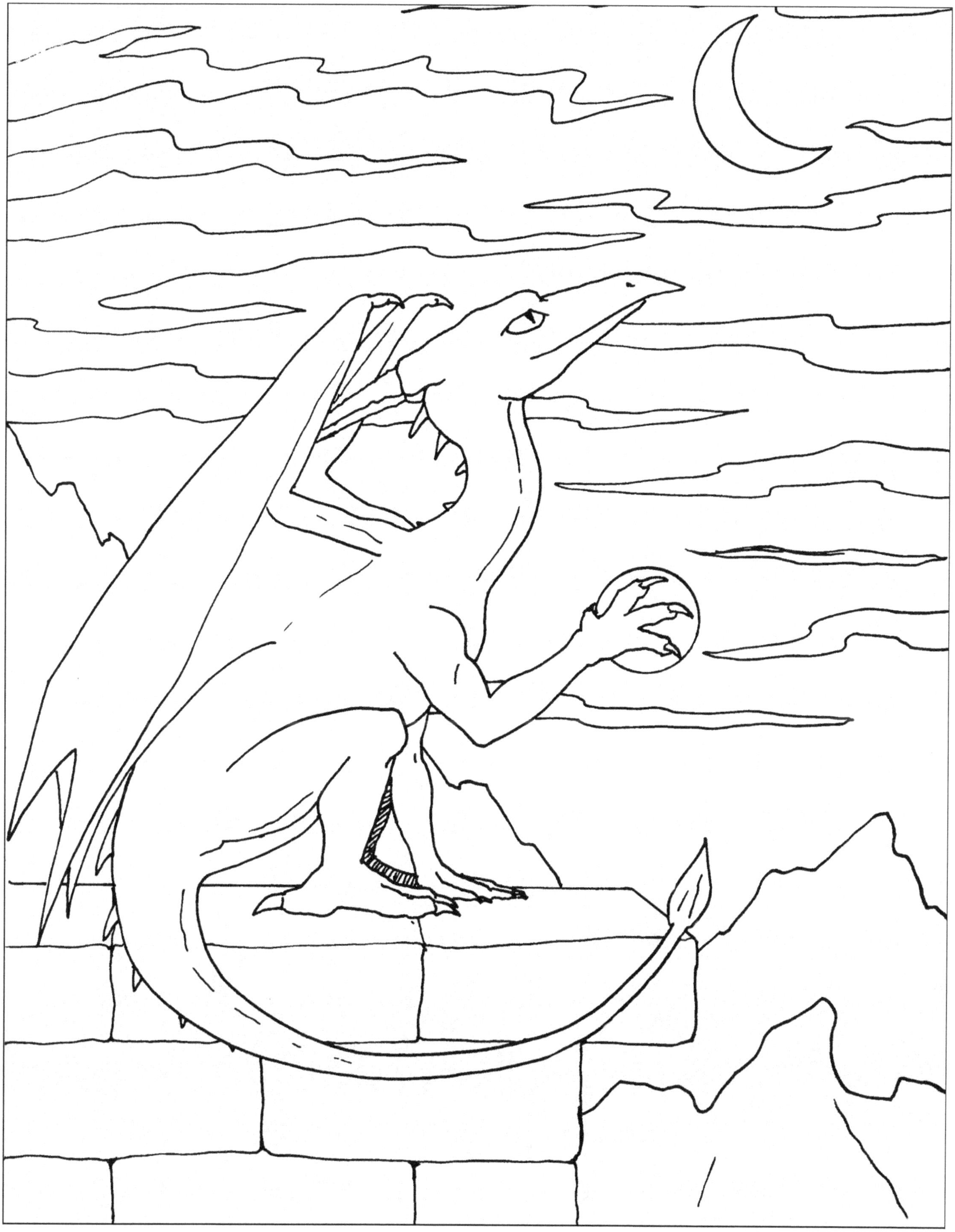

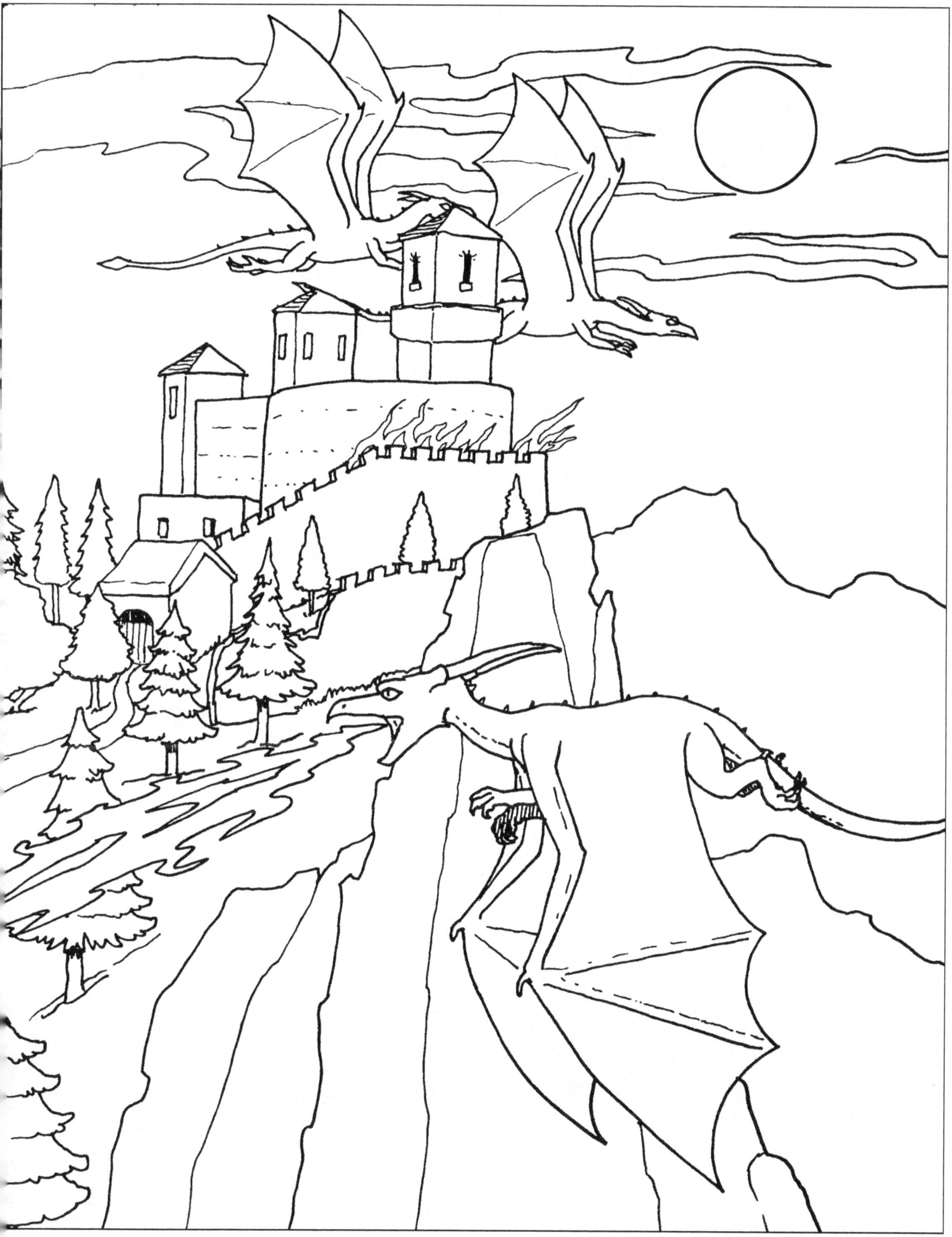

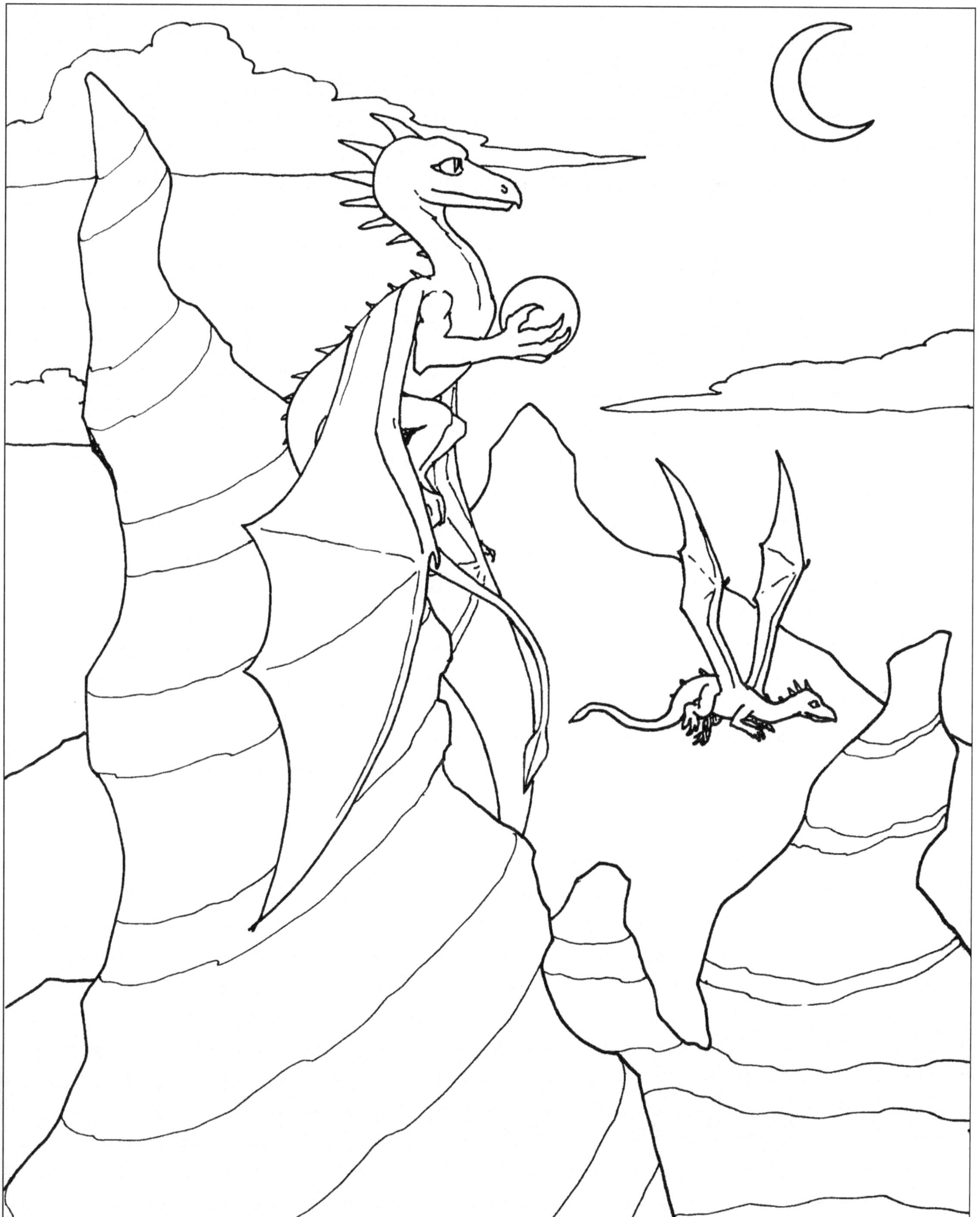

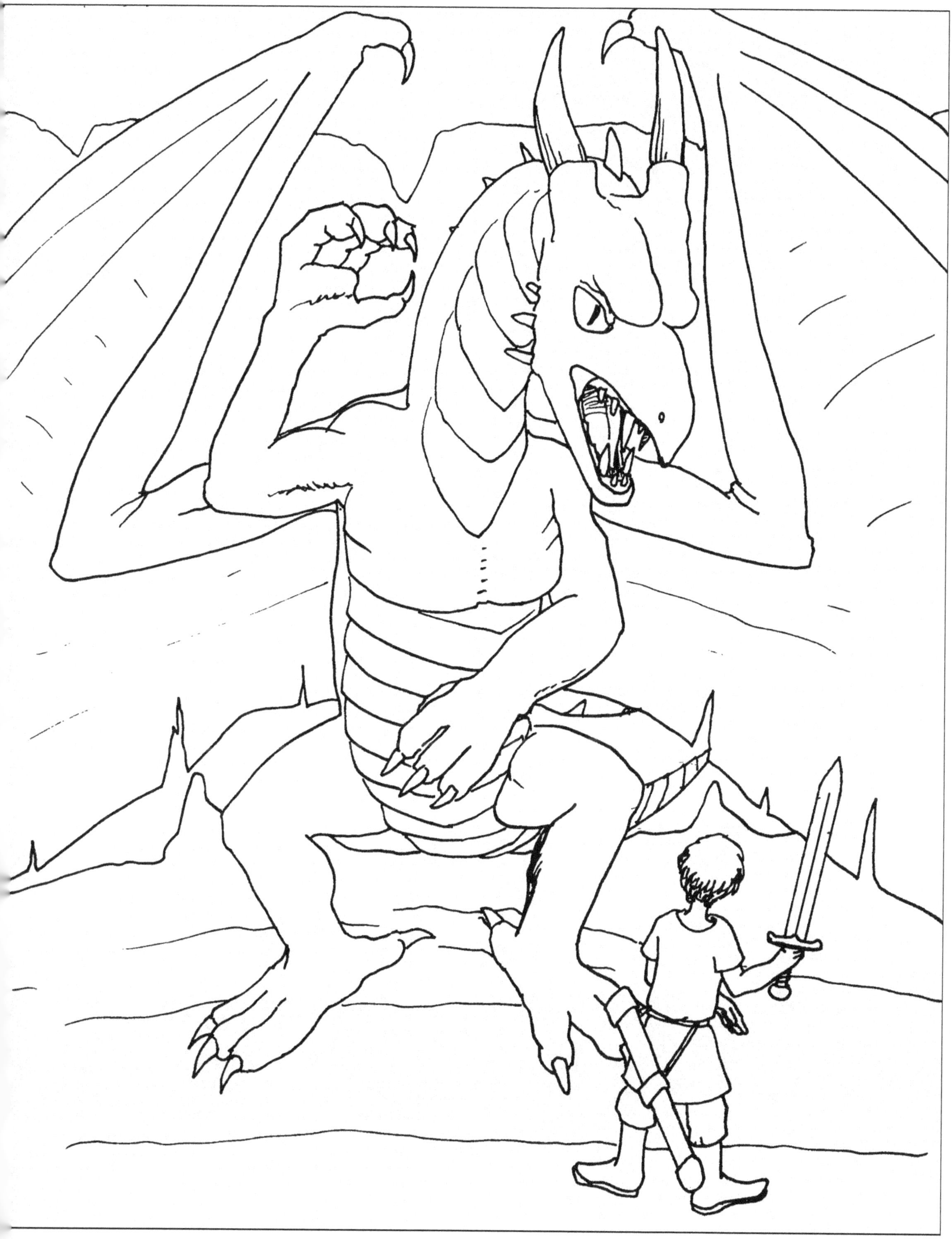

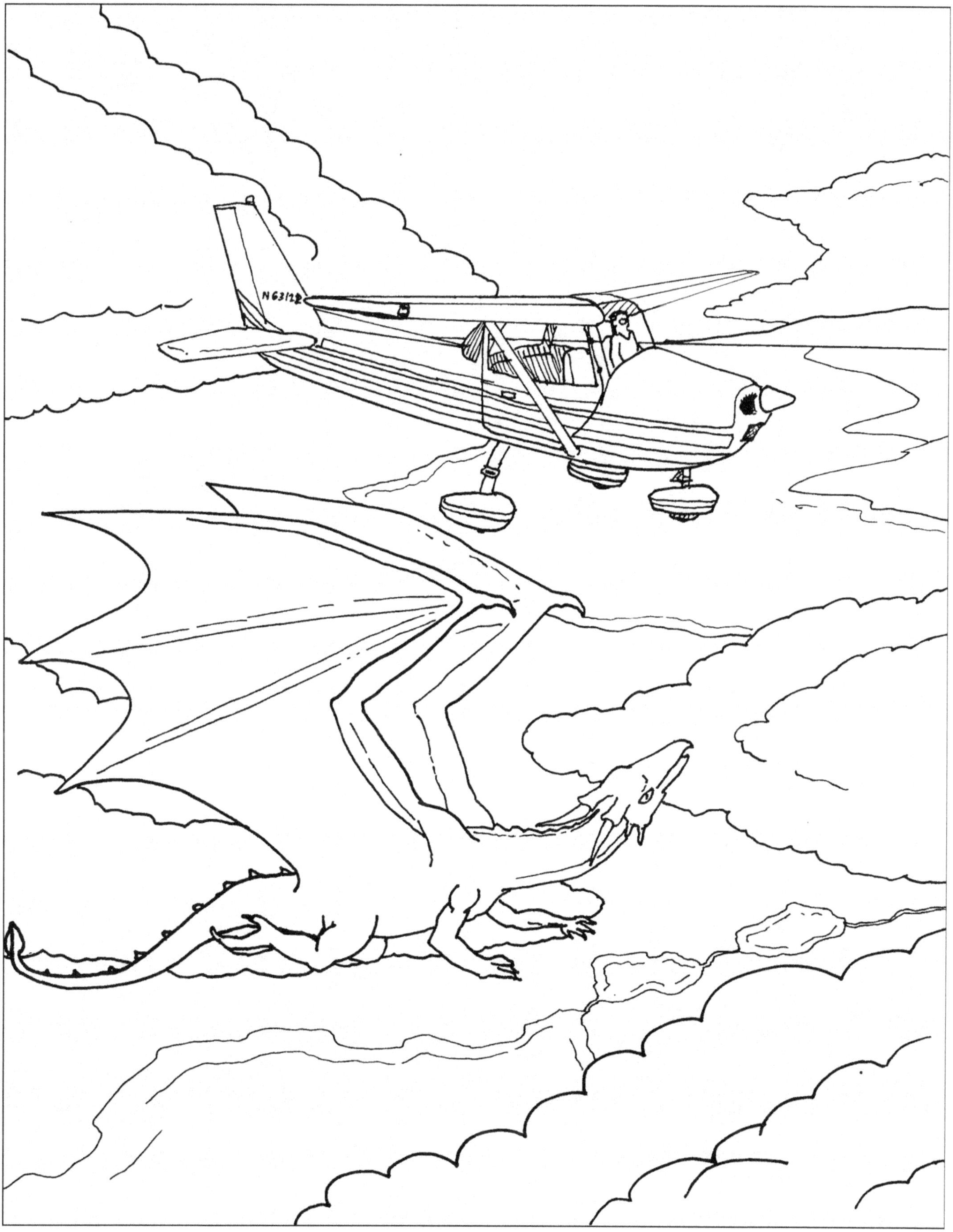

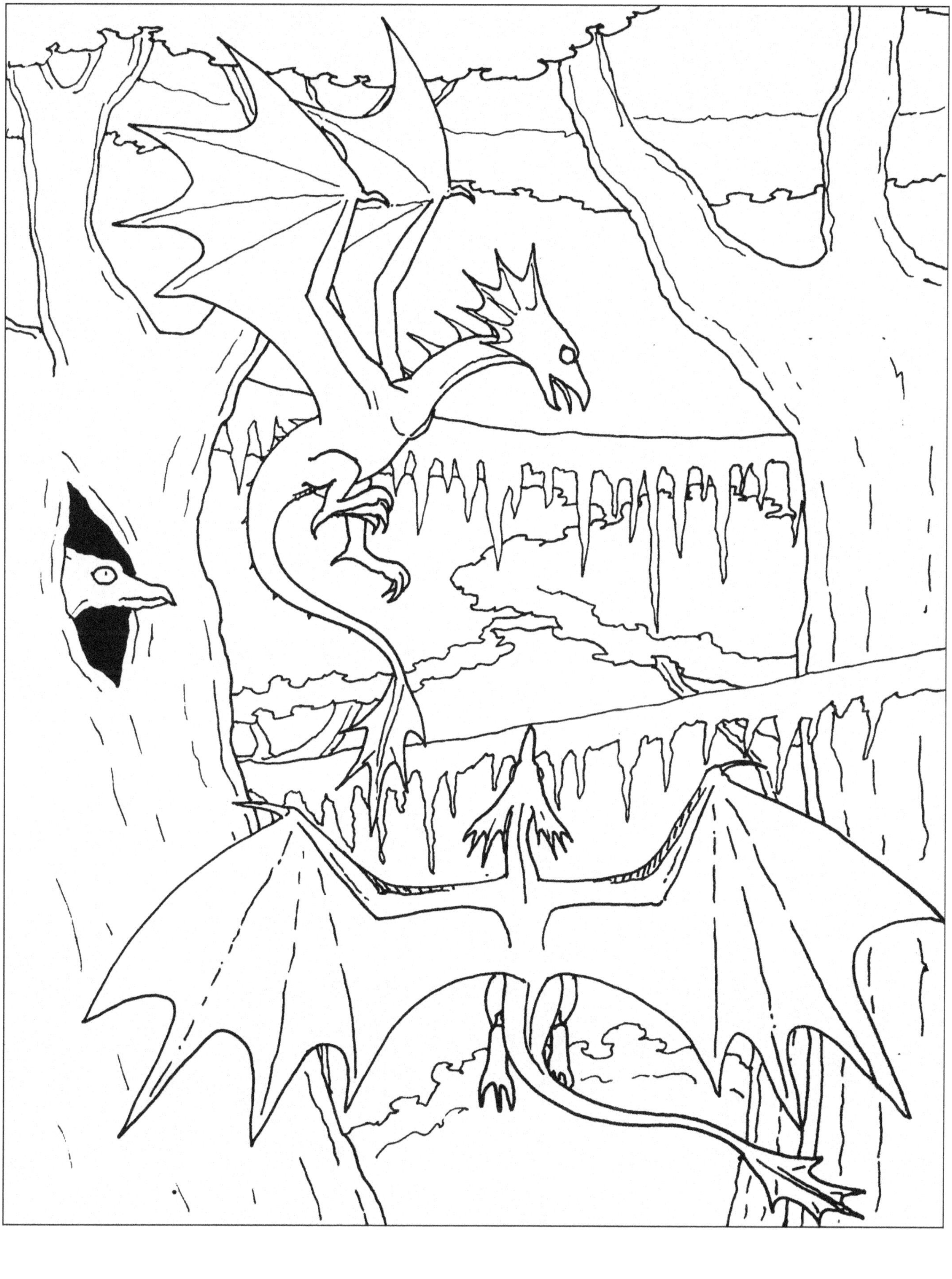

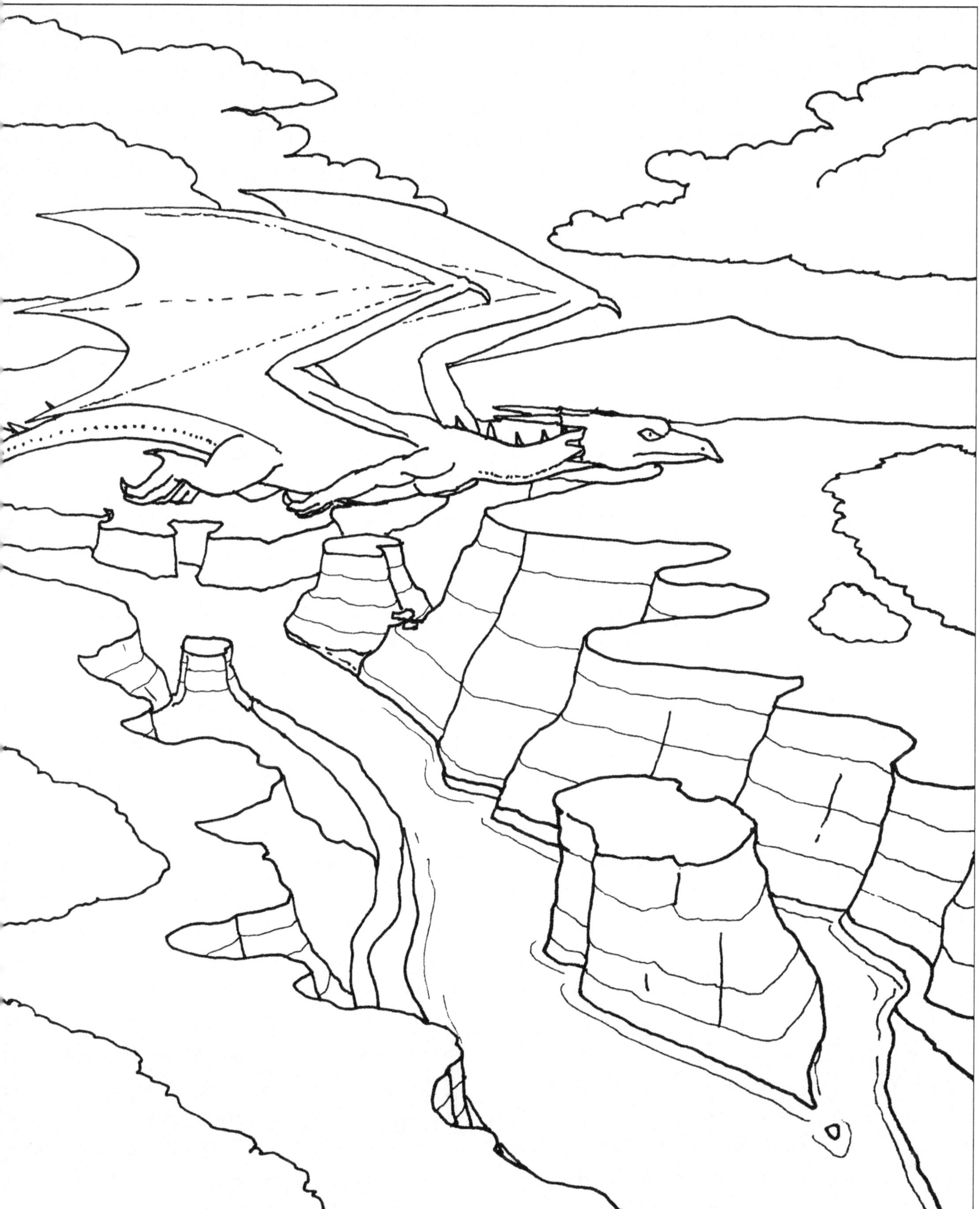

www.ingramcontent.com/pod-product-compliance
Lightning Source LLC
Chambersburg PA
CBHW080548190526
45169CB00007B/2681
9781530761524